IVY LANE REMEMBERED

Edited by

Doris Hughes

Publication Team

Joyce Beadle
Colin Graham
Jean Hastings
Nickie Young

CANTERBURY

1200 *(Canterbury Archaeological Trust, partly based on W. Urry)*

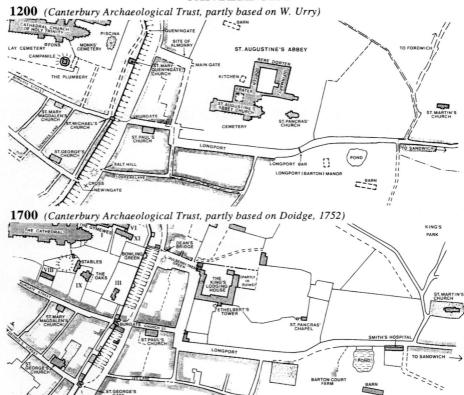

1700 *(Canterbury Archaeological Trust, partly based on Doidge, 1752)*

1994 *(Reproduced, with permission, from 1/10,000 Ordnance Survey, 1989)*

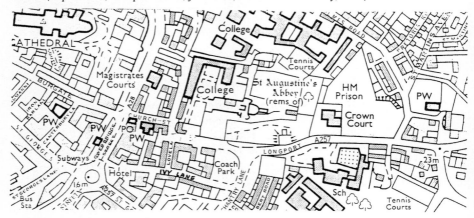

© *Crown Copyright*

IVY LANE REMEMBERED

"Ivy Lane is of special interest for it may well have once formed the final section of the Pilgrims Way from Dover to Canterbury. It is certainly far older than Chantry Lane, which terminates its eastern end, and it probably continued from there in an easterly direction to join the Pilgrims Way bridle-path, which still exists to the North of St Augustine's Road."
(Canterbury Conservation Study - 1979)

The jewel of this thoroughfare is The Hall, a 14th century Wealden house, once derelict, forsaken and so nearly demolished. It stands now as a triumph of one man's dream. That will be part of the remembrances of the 'Lane'.

Like many streets in Canterbury, Ivy Lane is numbered consecutively, 1 to 21 on north side and 35 to 63 on the south. The numbers in between are missing because the buildings were destroyed in the bombing of the Second World War or demolished later. It runs roughly east to west, and there are two turnings off on the northern side, a cul-de-sac, St Paul's Terrace, and Love Lane which connects to Longport. There is also a little yard, leading to the 'hidden houses', secreted at the rear of the gardens of Nos. 7 and 9 Longport. On the south side behind a door a small alley still exists between Nos. 55 and 56. This led to Moss's Square where stood six 'little cottages' as the local people called them. Until recently there was a third turning off Ivy Lane known as Union Row or Oak Alley as it connected Ivy Lane to Longport, passing the rear entrance of the Royal Oak public house. The cottages in Union Row were built by E Bridges in 1825, but demolished in 1978 to enlarge the car, coach and lorry park, established there by the Canterbury City Council on the site bombed in the last war.

Some twenty-four of the buildings in Ivy Lane are listed and the remainder contribute to the character of the City. It is no surprise to find this ancient way mentioned in the mediaeval rentals. It was here on the south side of Ivy Lane on the edge of the moat outside the City that John, son of Roger the cook, and Hamo, son of Roger, held land in 1166.

THE BOROUGH OF LONGPORT

The Abbot of St Augustine's and the citizens of Canterbury with the consent of King Henry III resolved the uncertainties of their boundaries and areas of jurisdiction in 1268. According to Hasted this agreement gave the boundary to run *"from the western gate of the cemetery of St Augustine's as far as the house of Henry the smith* (at the north end of Love Lane) *and from thence to the house of Nicholas de le Breton* (on the site of 52-57 Ivy Lane), *and then by the way called Loder's Lane* (Ivy Lane) *as far as New Street* (Lower Chantry Lane)*"*.

Land north of Ivy Lane and east of Love Lane was thus in the Manor of Longport and later in the Borough of Longport, which continued to be outside the normal jurisdiction of the City and within the County of Kent. This existed right through to the 19th century, when the census records refer separately to *"St Paul's in the City"* and *"St Paul's in the County"*.

In ancient times Ivy Lane was known as Lodderelane. As Dr William Urry tells us, *"at the bottom of the social scale there are beggars, who left a trace of themselves in the name of the alley outside Newingate* (later St George's) *which they must have haunted, called Beggars' Lane* (Lodderelane). *"* After 1221 the whole of the south side of the Lane, except a plot at the east end on Lower Chantry Lane, was held by the Abbey of St Augustine. In 1375 the Ivy Lane land was held by Henry Garnate who was bailiff of the City in 1384. In 1363 Lodderelane was known as Standfast Lane, after John Standfast who occupied a house on the site of the present 52-57 Ivy Lane in that period. Eight years on it became Wanree's Lane, from the Prior's Senechal (steward), William Wanere, who resided there.

William Oldfield, bellfounder, who made the bells for St Paul's Boughton Aluph, had a foundry in the Lane. In 1541, following the orders of Henry VIII, a sum was *"Payd to Oldfield bellfounder for putting owte Thomas Bekket from the Common Seale and gravyng agayn of the same"*. (Arch. Cant.xii,38) Thus was Becket's name removed from the Common Seal. By 1562 Wanree's Lane was already known as Bellfounder Lane.

It was during the 16th century that the Ive family came here, bequeathing their name to the Lane. The family had a heretic ancestor who was martyred in 1511 and buried in the Dane John without rites. Paul Ive, an engineer, wrote *The Practice of Fortification*. He went to King's School, where Christopher Marlowe attended, and it is thought that Marlowe had access to the text prior to publication, using some of it in his play *Tamburlaine*. Paul Ive built at least two fortifications in Ireland and, like Marlowe, was in Queen Elizabeth's secret service.

The 16th century brought an influx of Huguenot refugees into Canterbury. They were welcomed to the City, and given the crypt of the Cathedral in which to worship; a service in French is still held in the crypt every Sunday at 3.00 pm. They brought with them the art of brocade weaving which stimulated the local trade. In the City records of 1560 we are told that a lady walking along Ivy Lane at 6.00 am relates how *"all the time poor neighbours were spinning at their door"* (making thread to sell to the weavers in the town).

UP AND DOWN THE LANE

"The haphazard relationship of building to building established over the centuries is the essential characterisitc of Ivy Lane. Building lines, eaves and ridge heights, roof pitches and architectural style show little uniformity but all are bound together by a harmonious blend of traditional materials and the compatibility of the building forms of previous generations."
(Canterbury Conservation Study - 1979).

It is worth a walk along each side of the Lane, pausing here and there to rummage for things associated with the buildings, the shades of persons past and to remember those in our own time.

When coal was the prime source for heating and cooking in the home then the coal-cellar was essential. For some houses access for deliveries was by the coal-hole set in the pavement and placed conveniently above the cellars. Here the coal-man could empty his sacks without going through the house.

Several houses have foot scrapers set in the wall by the cottage doors, a memory of times before tarmac, when the mud of the Lane could be left at the street door.

Many houses have footscrapers. This one is outside No. 3 Ivy Lane
Photo: J. B.

Coal hole covers on the pavement outside Nos. 54 & 57A Ivy Lane
Photo: Joyce Beadle

THE HOUSES - NORTH SIDE

Nos. 1-6

ENSIGNE PLACE (1-4) was built in 1856 on land owned by Isaac Berry, replacing earlier tenements on this site. Isaac Berry also owned Nos. 15-21 Ivy Lane and the land behind those properties. He is described as a licensed hawker in the 1861 census when, aged fifty-one, he lived at No. 19. Three cottages, Nos. 19-21 were for some years known as 'Berry's Cottages'.

The two cottages (5-6) are older and were built around 1800 on a strip of land which in the 13th century was held from the Abbey by Agnes, daughter of Wydon and Eastrilde. After the dissolution it was owned by the Hales family together with the site of Ensigne Place (1-4).

Mrs Glenys Edwards retired to No. 2 cottage in 1977 after having been licensee of 'The Old City of Canterbury' in Dover Street for about 38 years.

3

Ensigne Place built 1856 - Photo: J. B.

Sally and Brian King came to live at No. 3 Ensigne Place in 1969. The house was a wedding gift from the bride's father. The house had a cold water tap in the kitchen and electricity, but no bathroom. Sally King:- *"We heard that No. 4 was for sale, it had a dilapidation order on it, there was no water or electricity and was full of mice. We had the two houses knocked into one."* (Note the footscraper without a door where No. 4 had been.) *"It took over five months to do this. We were left with the shell of the house. When we came in 1969 Mrs West lived in No. 5 and Mrs Foster in No. 6 and she had gaslighting."* They established a chiropody practice at these premises which was carried on by Sally King. Brian King was a chiropodist at Guy's hospital in London. He also worked for the Kent and Canterbury hospital for thirteen years. In 1993 they ceased the chiropody practice in Ivy Lane.

Nos. 7-13

These cottages are on the frontage of a plot of land which ran back to the old vicarage behind St. Paul's church. The oldest of these is No. 7 (Carolean Cottage) which is a two-bay mediaeval cottage. It was extended some six feet to the west in the 17th century to incorporate a chimney at the west end. It is the cottage which is mentioned in the grant of this land to the City in 1543. On the side wall is a plaque with the date 1627 and an upside down heart, either side of which are initials, now hardly readable. It is supposed that

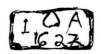

Wall plaque No.7 Ivy Lane

the date may have indicated either a change of ownership or reconstruction, since the building is considered to be older than the inscription. There are some fine old timbers inside, and a noteworthy feature is the 'cat slide' roof at the rear of the house.

Gilkes Masters, who held this lease early in the 17th century, obtained permission from the City in 1631 to build on the Ivy Lane frontage and it was shortly after that the existing No. 13 was built. No doubt Masters also built between Nos. 7 and 13 but these were replaced in the 18th century by an oast. The original plot was divided in 1724 into two leases, one covering the cottage on the lane frontage, the other covering the ground at the back which was later to become St Paul's Terrace. The Terrace first appears in Steven's Directory of 1889 and mentions ten houses and St Paul's School. The school has gone but the houses remain.

The entrance to St Paul's Terrace is of long standing. Early in the 18th century there was an archway over it with a room above, some sixteen feet square and forming part of No. 7 Ivy Lane, but this had been pulled down by the early 19th century.

From the late 19th century onwards No. 7 had a succession of shops; from grocer (1882 Mr Spicer) to greengrocer (Elizabeth Green 1891) to General Stores (Henry Bradford 1897/98 and S T Bailey 1911/12). In 1925 Charles Ilott the 'snob' (boot repairer) had 7A and later he took over the whole house. He was there until 1955 and is well remembered in the locality, having been in the shop over 30 years.

Carolean Cottage No. 7 Ivy Lane - Photo: Bill Avis

Nos. 8-12 are on the site of the 18th century oast mentioned above. The premises were leased from the City Council in 1832 for £19 p.a. by Henry Laming, bricklayer, and son William, silk weaver and freeman by birth. Included in the lease were another three messuages No. 7 (Carolean Cottage) and No. 13, a 17th century house, divided at the time into two. Laming demolished the oast and two dwellings and built the present Nos. 8 to 12 in their place. In 1832 he set himself up as the landlord of the Fox and Hounds at No. 13 which continued as a public house until 1908. In 1838 Laming purchased the resulting seven dwellings from the City for £507.15s.

In 1693 No. 12 was a public house known as 'The Compasses', later called 'The Carpenters Arms'. According to the 1851 census John Roberts, gardener, lived there with his wife and two children. Bat and Trap, an old Kentish pub game was played in the garden at one time.

Mrs Hannah Rose, the first wife of Sir Alec Rose lived in No. 13. She tells us: *"I lived from the age of eighteen in Monastery Street. In 1958 I moved to 13 Ivy Lane with my four children, two sons and two daughters. No. 13 was a wonderful house it has old oak beams. It was an old ale house. There is a beer cellar underneath where they kept the barrels. There was a bollard outside where the old farmers used to come and tie up. In actual fact my grandfather used to tie up outside there. He was a farmer in Littlebourne and he came into Canterbury about twice a week. He tied up outside and had his glass of ale before doing his deliveries in Canterbury."*

Alec Rose was born in Canterbury on 13 July 1908, went to Simon Langton School, and sang in St Paul's choir. Mrs Rose continues:- *" He went to Canada and when he returned he worked in his father's haulage business. He was working there when we married in 1931."* His father was killed in the 1942 raid whilst living at 4a Lady Wootton's Green and *"During the war Alec was in the Navy on the Russian and Atlantic convoys. I saw him about four times in six years! Alec did not live at No.13, as he was building a boat* (Lively Lady) *in Ramsgate Harbour. At this time we were just on the point of divorce."*

In 1967/68 Alec Rose sailed his yacht *Lively Lady* single-handed round the world in eleven months, a feat only surpassed by Francis Chichester, who made the same voyage in seven months. Hannah Rose recalls *"Alec took the journey back to a wonderful welcome in this country."*

Nos. 13A-14 (and Nos. 1-4 Love Lane)

The corner site, built on in 1888, had been a garden for centuries until Thomas Francis Cozens early in the 19th century used it as a builder's yard. He lived at No. 6 Love Lane. He built Nos. 7-13 Love Lane and No. 6 Longport around 1826. He was the main contractor for the extension of St Paul's church in the 1840's. Later in the 19th century the business was continued by his son John Francis Cozens who lived at 12 Longport and used the site of St Paul's Terrace as a builder's yard. The original builder's premises (No. 14) was next to the present No. 13. In 1888 No. 14 was demolished and

Farley Cottages were built to face on to Love Lane. In the meantime the number fourteen had been allocated to what is now Wickenden's builder's yard. By 1973 The Samaritans had moved into these premises from above the Pilch & Collard office, later Chaucer Hair, and here they remained until March 1990 when they set up office in Northgate. This (13A) is now the offices for Consult Group Ltd and Consult Group (GB) Ltd, whose concern is industrial research.

Nos. 12 and 13 Ivy Lane - Photo: B. A.

THE WAREHOUSE

The fine Victorian warehouse at the junction of Ivy Lane and Love Lane occupies a site where in the 15th century, Alice, the widow of John Monyn, had her mansion house, courtyard, cookhouse and a piece of ground (on the corner) called Bassetisland, which is also mentioned in a 13th century rental of St Augustine's property of Longport. The warehouse (20 Love Lane) was rebuilt in 1888 by Taylors of Canterbury, an old established local firm. They were in business as fruiterers and seedsmen in the City for over two hundred years. The warehouse was built as a corn store. It replaced Harman's corn stores that stood on the site in 1882. Ruth Taylor said *"It was built by my grandfather. When my father was going to sell it somebody said that they had never seen a floor built like it. It has very thick oak boards tongued and grooved with steel"*.

After Taylor's finished trading in 1958 the building was in use as a builders and decorator's merchant (Brewers). It was they who built on to the rear end of the building the present loading bay. Later it became a restaurant and wholefood shop, then an antique market and Latimer's furniture store, but now it stands empty (1994). The small building east of the warehouse is still shown as No. 14 on the current O.S. map. It was once the stables for No. 11 Longport, the door to the hay loft is still clearly visible. It was within memory a forge and blacksmith's. Mr John Adkins was employed here by Wickenden's as a blacksmith and metal work engineer. It was he who made the fine wrought iron gates, with spider and fly motif and 'The Forge' worked into the fascia above.

Taylor Bros. Warehouse c1930 - Photo courtesy of Ruth Taylor

The Forge - Photo: B. A.

Nos. 15 to 18 Ivy Lane - Photo: B. A.

Mr R Wickenden senior pays tribute to this now retired craftsman. *"He is a skilful man. He made the cross and candlesticks for St Thomas's church, he also designed and made the wrought-iron work behind the bar and the window grilles, which contain a cricket motif, in the Leslie Ames Pavilion at the Kent County Cricket Ground".*

In the 1930's the yard provided a back entrance to 11 Longport where on the ground floor the KCC dental clinic was held. From 1921 to 1958 the yard was the premises of George Coombs & Sons. They were carpenters, joiners and builders. It then passed to Wickendens who have occupied it ever since. By walking a short pace or two into Wickenden's yard it is possible to glimpse the roofs of the 'hidden cottages'. These stand at the end of the gardens of Nos. 7 and 8 Longport. Uninhabited, they are the 'one-up, one-down' labourers' cottages of an earlier time, possibly late 18th or early 19th century.

Nos. 15-18

These were built by Isaac Berry in the mid 19th century and he still owned them later in the century. In 1434 John Berton had his tenement and barn on the site of Nos. 15-18. There was an oast owned by John Gillman in 1803 on the site of Nos. 19-21. Five oasts stood in Ivy Lane by the end of the 18th century.

In 1697 Celia Fiennes had noted the great hopyards on the road from Faversham to Canterbury. By a Charter of George III in 1766, a weekly toll-free hop market was set up in Canterbury to operate every Wednesday, which made the City a centre of the hop trade in this area of Kent. It was Defoe early in the 18th century who stressed that *"the*

The former Co-Op Bakery - Photo: T. Dowse

The Old Bakehouse, 1993 - Photo: B. A.

great wealth and increase of the City of Canterbury is from the surprizing increase of the hop-grounds all around the place". Even Cobbett mentioned (1832) *"this year, while the hops are so bad in most parts, they are not so bad about Canterbury."* Maps before 1800 show hops growing on the land on both sides of Lower Chantry Lane.

From 1882 until 1915 Ralph Thomas traded as a bootmaker at No. 18, and it was at No. 18 that Wickendens, the builders, lived and carried on their business before the war. During the war they rented the garden of 11 Longport from the Misses Young, and here they grew vegetables, built an air raid shelter, and created a small children's playground.

THE OLD BAKEHOUSE

Between Nos. 18 and 19 is the Old Bakehouse, a modern office development by 'Townscape'. This was skillfully and imaginatively designed; set back from the Lane it fits well into the street scene. This was the site of the old Co-op Bakery from 1923 until at least 1967. During the war the First Aid Post was at the Bakery. After development it was the main office for Townscape, they have now gone and the building is occupied by Sinclairs, the solicitors, and Clyde Design Partnership. The latter provide a range of services in Architecture and Interior Design, Civil, Structural and Engineering Services and Quantity Surveying. They use sophisticated technology, and the practice is highly computerised. They operate nationally and abroad.

No. 19-23

As early as 1861 No. 22 was a public house named 'The Brewery Tap' which stood next to 'The Eagle Brewery'. In 1882 Mr Henry Doyle had a retail beer business at these premises, which by 1893 had reverted to a public house taking the former name of 'The Brewery Tap'. By 1897 it was again a beer retailing business, but in 1904 this once more became a public house known as 'The Duke of York' which remained until 1929, after which it became a private house. Canterbury City Council demolished this building in 1978 along with a row of near derelict houses in Union Row.

Nos. 19 to 21 Ivy Lane - Photo: B. A.

Amey's Works, 1975 - Photo: Paul Crampton

*Amey' Workers, L to R: Johnnie Boylett, Ron Parker, Frank Fleet,
Edward (Harry) Crampton, Horace Meers - Photo: P. C.*

No. 23

In 1861 John Browning, maltman, and Dan French, sawyer, lived at this address. By 1882 Stevens Directory gives Henry Royle, beer retailer. From 1888 the premises were occupied by J Coombes, painter, who is recorded as living at this address until 1939. The name then disappears.

The Eagle Brewery was adjacent to No. 23. This had gone by 1889, and been replaced by Holden's mineral water manufactory and J D Maxted's Creameries. By 1893 Holden's had gone and Maxted's had been replaced by 'Canterbury Creameries'; by 1894 this firm had also gone. It is likely that part of this site was used when the Payne Smith school was built in the 1890's. A large building, possibly Collard's oast, that survived the 1942 bombing in this area was the works of Amey & Son, blind-makers. Amey's not only made blinds for shops but also other canvas products. Mr Edward Crampton started at Amey's in the 1920's as an errand boy and rose to become a director of the firm. He retired in 1974. He has said *"We used to make coal bags and pockets for the hops. When I first came to the firm we were the only shop-blind makers in Kent."* During the 1939-45 war the firm was specially busy making blackout blinds, which were already being produced for x-ray departments of hospitals and operating theatres. Large canvas covers were also made for goods vehicles. The most bizarre item produced was canvas saddles or covers for the poultry, particularly for the female turkeys, to protect them in the breeding season when they become very vulnerable to the cold.

Looking towards the site of Union Row (Oak Alley) and Nos. 23 and 24 Ivy Lane - Photo: B. A.

The site of Nos. 24 to 34 Ivy Lane, present Safeways car park - Photo: B.A.

Nos. 35 to 40 Ivy Lane - Photo: B. A.

THE HOUSES - SOUTH SIDE

Nos. 24-29

This site was thought to have been held first by the Hospitals of St John's Northgate (1352) and then St Nicholas, Harbledown (1363). Unfortunately, the records were destroyed in the last war but summaries of these lost deeds were found in *"Three Archiespiscopal Hospitals"* (1785) and confirm the holding. By the 18th century the two hospitals shared this property and by the 19th century St John's owned all of it. They later sold it to the City. This century there were fourteen cottages on the plot, six cottages (Nos. 24-29) on the Ivy Lane frontage and eight on the Lower Chantry Lane frontage. In 1882 Smith's stables were at No. 29. In 1925 Nos. 24-27 Ivy Lane were demolished and Nos. 28 and 29 joined into one cottage with No. 29A made into a garage. These were destroyed by enemy action in 1942.

Nos. 30-34

These occupied the site of the house of Alice of Cirencester, the rent from which was given to Hamo Doge in 1266 as part of his endowment of the Chantry.

A shop stood here in 1375 but by 1434 it was an open garden and continued as open space until 1800 when five cottages were built on the Lane frontage. 18th century maps show it as part of the hop-field to the south and when George Young, described as *"of the Chantery"*, purchased the adjoining property to the west in 1658 he already owned this plot and the field to the south of it. The cottages Nos. 30-34 were destroyed by enemy action in the war.

It was here that A.H. Amey & Son , Blind and Canvas Cover makers, had premises in temporary buildings after the war. The main works were on the north side of the Lane. When Safeways purchased their present site in the 1980's it included the land on which these cottages had stood. The *Kentish Gazette* reported in 12 February 1982:- *"New houses facing Ivy Lane to be built as part of the Safeway development, should fit in with the character of the old street."* The new development is still awaited. The site is now used as a staff car park by Safeways, giving an uninviting aspect to an ancient and historic thoroughfare.

Nos. 35-40

A mediaeval building stood here before the existing villas were built around 1917. The age of this building is not known but there was apparently a shop here in 1375 and what was described as a tenement in 1434. Thomas Palmer, husbandman, held the lease in 1591/2 and paid the City £1 a year. Richard Gaunt in his accounts called it *"all that messuage or tenement and one garden thereto adioyninge."* In 1560 the lease had been held by John Morrys for 6s.8d. p.a. and Thomas Palmer, who married Rose Morrys at St Paul's in 1577, must have inherited the lease by right of his wife. He was churchwarden of St Paul's 1591-4 and 1597-1601. The lease continued in the Palmer family until 1625 when it was assigned to John Wright of All Saints, clothworker. In 1639 George Young took over the lease at an increased rent of 26s.8d p.a. and in 1658 he purchased the freehold from the City for £20.

George Young already owned the adjoining plot to the east and that to the west which probably included *"The Hall"*. The resulting block of properties was still in one ownership in the 19th century when it was owned by John Aris who was Clerk to the

Justices and lived at Ivy Lane House, now part of the Chaucer Hotel.

Nos. 40A-41

The frontage of these cottages could be 14th century but the rear extension is much later. No. 40A was reduced in width in 1917, when Nos. 35-40 were built, to provide a space for a side passage; at the same time the roof was raised to give a second floor. These buildings could have been on the same plot as that of 'The Hall' and may have been ancillary to it; the old boundary line of 'The Hall' plot appears to have been on the line of the west wall of No. 40 Ivy Lane.

Miss Josephine Carroll lived in 40A, probably the smallest cottage in the Lane, all her life. She was Auntie Josie to Violet Davison and Eileen Davies and they remember her as a hard worker, who had been employed at the hospital in Longport for many years, when Miss Annie Purchas was matron. After the hospital moved in the 1930's Auntie Josie took work at the Baker's Temperance Hotel (present Chaucer Hotel). Later she was forced to give up work because of ill health. Mrs Alison France with her husband came to manage the newly renovated Chaucer Hotel in 1957, and inherited the staff, including Auntie Josie. Mrs France has this to say:- *"She was Irish and she was a chambermaid and she was simply marvellous - everything was just perfect with Josie. She used to tell such wonderful tales. All the guests loved her. They would ask 'Are we on Josie's floor?'."*

Mr Richardson, father of Violet and Eileen, was born in this house. He died aged eightyfour in 1978. His wife had a greengrocer's shop in the Lane while he worked at Mount's farm.

Violet speaks of Auntie Josie *"We're a family that's brought up to think that doctors mean nothing, and we just got over whatever we had, and my Auntie Josie - she'd never go to a doctor. She wasn't registered with a doctor at all"*. It was this obstinacy and determination never to have a doctor or leave her little house that was to end in tragedy when she died of hyperthermia in the severe winter of 1985. So passed one of the colourful characters of the Lane.

The house was now for sale and was bought by the architect Mr James Bamford. It was beautifully and inge-

No. 40A Ivy Lane - Photo: Margaret Miller

niously restored. The present owner Margaret Miller has this to say:- *"The peace of this tiny house produces an atmosphere of great tranquillity which affects all our friends who stay there. Visitors in particular find it irresistible to stroke the ancient pillars and beams. The original front door was made into the kitchen table. The old wattle and daub walls are safely covered in to protect them but I am considering exposing some and covering them with glass. During restoration we were advised by the archaeologists and conservation officer that the original building and stairs were around six hundred years old. Later the sloping roof was squared off to give a full upper floor. We are keeping carefully the old wooden lid of the copper."*

THE HALL No. 42 *(Nos. 42-46 old numbering)*

The Hall is a 14th century Wealden house, timber framed with an open hall of two bays and a two storey bay at each end. It has an all-over hipped roof. Originally it would have had a central fire, the smoke going out from ventilator tiles in the roof. Smokey rafters were found in the roof timbers. The fire would have been kept in at night and covered with a pottery curfew. The Black Book of St Augustine's Abbey tells us that *"In the time of Abbot George Penshurst (1431-1457) William Purden, chaplain, was granted for life a messuage in Loderers' Lane at a rent of 20s."* Architectural details suggest that it might be part of the Doges Chantry, but positive proof is lacking. Dr W. Urry states in a letter to Mr James Hobbs, one time owner, *"Your house is elusive. It has always fascinated me since I was very young, but I have never been able to identify it satisfactorily in the archives."*

In 1600 The Hall was floored over, a back chimney inserted and a 17th century fireplace put in with a spiral staircase beside it. By the 19th century The Hall was divided into four cottages inhabited in 1851 by twenty-five occupants. In 1960 these cottages, condemned and due to be demolished. were saved by Mr Sean Fielding, an author, formerly a Fleet Street journalist and editor of *The Tatler*. The *Kentish Gazette* 4th March 1960 reported *"Mr and Mrs Sean Fielding were visiting their son John at King's School, and found these 500-year-old cottages and breathed a new life into them at a time when they were about to fall down."*

In April 1960 Mr Anthony Swaine, architect, was commissioned and work commenced. On 4 March 1960 the *Kentish Gazette* reported:- *"Mr S Fielding hopes to spend Christmas there with his wife and three sons"*. Much restoration was needed and use was made of suitable materials from elsewhere, all faithfully recorded by Mr Swaine to avoid misleading future historians. The front door came from Durlock Grange, Minster in Thanet, where it had been the back door - note the old iron lock plate. A full list of the source of the restoration materials may be seen in the *Parish of St Martin and St Paul Canterbury, Historical Essays in Memory of James Hobbs*. The restoration of The Hall was the inspiration of Mr Fielding and it is to him that we owe a debt of gratitude. Unhappily he did not live there long as he died in March 1963. By 1975 the owner was Mr James Hobbs. He was an early member of the Oaten Hill and District Society, a great friend and supporter of the Canterbury Archaeological Society, and a parishioner of St Martin and St Paul's. His interest in local history and friendship with Dr. Urry resulted in bringing to light much of the history of Longport and Ivy Lane. We are indebted to him for much of the material used in this booklet. Tragically, James Hobbs died in a car accident in 1979. He was much loved locally and the book mentioned above was published in his memory.

Mr J S R Baxter, the ear, nose and throat consultant at the Kent and Canterbury Hospital, and his wife Patty were recent owners of The Hall. It was whilst living there

No. 42 The Hall (c1920/30) - Photo: Neil Mattingley

The Hall, interior view - Photo courtesy Cluttons

that they bought a house in Romania that has been adapted as an orphanage for child victims of the unhappy events in that country. Already the first children are in residence there. The Charity 'Hope Romania' continues to raise funds to maintain and extend this caring project.

No. 43 'Chantry House' *(47 to 50 old numbering)*

Four shops stood on this site in 1434, two of which were owned by the Abbey of St John's Hospital, Northgate, and the other two by St Nicholas Hospital Harbledown. Those held by St John's had previously been held by William Benet, a leading citizen of Canterbury and seven times elected Bailiff between 1415 and 1444, the year in which he died. In the Hospitals' muniments were two deeds: one, dated 1430, among the St John's documents, in which John Lovel, cleric, and others, feoffs of the late Henry Webb, granted two shops in St Paul's to William Benet: and the other, dated 1424, in the St Nicholas chest, in which John Lovel and others granted two shops in Standfast Lane to John Newman and others. This latter deed was endorsed *"Eydence of two houses in Ive Lane Cant-bur."* The Rector of St George's, John Lovel, who died in 1438, was buried in St George's church but his memorial brass has been removed to St Peter's church. His connection with the Abbey is not known although, like Hamo Doge, he gave some books to the library there.

Later there was some exchange of land between the Hospitals both of which sold their properties on this site in 1960. No. 46 was sold by St John's to become the garage of The Hall and Nos. 47-50 were sold by St Nicholas to become the site of the present 'Chantry House'. In 1960 the purchaser of the properties was the builder, Mr Robert Wickenden. The near derelict houses beside The Hall were demolished, and on the site

The Hall and site of Nos. 47, 48, 49 and 50 Ivy Lane (1962). Prior to building of Chantry House
Photo: Shena Fielding

Mr Wickenden built a modern 'Hall' house. The architects were Dudley Marsh & Son. The large 'open plan' ground floor room has a central spiral staircase, enclosed in a brick half-drum, the pillar and metal treads of which were designed and made by the blacksmith, John Adkins. The staircase is placed where in a mediaeval house the central fire would have been. This modern house fits snugly into the surroundings.

The Wickendens came to live in Ivy Lane at No.18 in the 1930's. Mrs Wickenden, who is of Huguenot descent, is pleased to think that land hereabout was once in the ownership of her ancestors. The building business started by Robert Wickenden senior, thrived and there are many properties around Canterbury

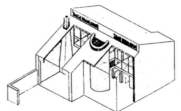

Rear plan of Chantry House (1966)
Courtesy of R Wickenden

where the firm has worked. Their work on the renovation of the Leslie Ames stand at the Kent County Cricket ground included a novel feature, which was the introduction of boxes. These had already been a feature of football ground stands, but were now introduced for the first time into the cricket pavilion. Another innovation was the revolutionary design of the wicket covers. The old and heavy canvas covers were burdensome to use. Wickenden's produced a perspex cover on wheels that was both light and easily removable. They received orders for these from other cricket clubs throughout Britain.

Chantry House - Photo: B. A.

No.51A and 51

Alderman John Nutt, who was Mayor of Canterbury in 1582, held this plot of the City and in his will left it to his son William Nutt, Counsellor at Law. He described it as *"my house and garden with appurtenances ... called the man of Warr"*. The property was later held by Alderman Southwell whose daughter married in 1639 Joy Starr, hosier of Ashford, who thereby inherited it. Comfort Starr, the brother of Joy, sailed with his family from Sandwich on the ship *Hercules* for New England in 1635 and became one of the earliest benefactors of Harvard, the first college (1638) in America. His son Comfort was, in 1650, one of the seven incorporators. This son, the Rev Comfort Starr, who was eleven years old when the family sailed from Sandwich, graduated at Harvard in 1647 and returned to England to become a Minister of the gospel at Carlisle during the Commonwealth but, being ejected in 1647, he moved south, first to Sandhurst, Kent and then to St Paul's Canterbury. His son was buried at St Paul's in 1679 and his second wife died in 1680. Joy Starr continued to have the house in Ivy Lane until his death in 1681 and it seems not unlikely that his nephew, the Rev. Comfort Starr, stayed there during the time he was in St Paul's parish.

The present house appears in the St Paul's Register in 1635 as a public house called 'The Ship'. It closed in 1700. There were many owners over the years and at one stage it seems to have incorporated an oast, on land at the rear. On 15th November 1831 there is a Burghmote Minute recording that John Deakney, retailer in beer, would be *"tolerated to carry on Trade, he having served His Majesty in the Royal Navy, paying fees accustomed"*, and John Deakney became the landlord of the public house named 'The Navy Arms' at 51 Ivy Lane. In the 1871 census return, the innkeeper is given as Mrs Susanna Gilbey, a widow with three daughters, the eldest, seventeen, being the

51A and 51 Ivy Lane - Photo: B. A.

IVY LANE ~ 1873

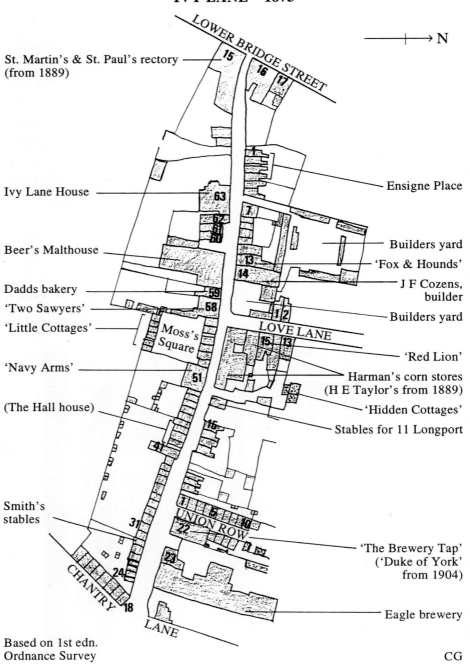

St. Martin's & St. Paul's rectory (from 1889)

Ivy Lane House

Beer's Malthouse

Dadds bakery

'Two Sawyers'

'Little Cottages'

'Navy Arms'

(The Hall house)

Smith's stables

Ensigne Place

Builders yard

'Fox & Hounds'

J F Cozens, builder

Builders yard

'Red Lion'

Harman's corn stores (H E Taylor's from 1889)

'Hidden Cottages'

Stables for 11 Longport

'The Brewery Tap' ('Duke of York' from 1904)

Eagle brewery

Based on 1st edn. Ordnance Survey

CG

22

IVY LANE ~ 1994

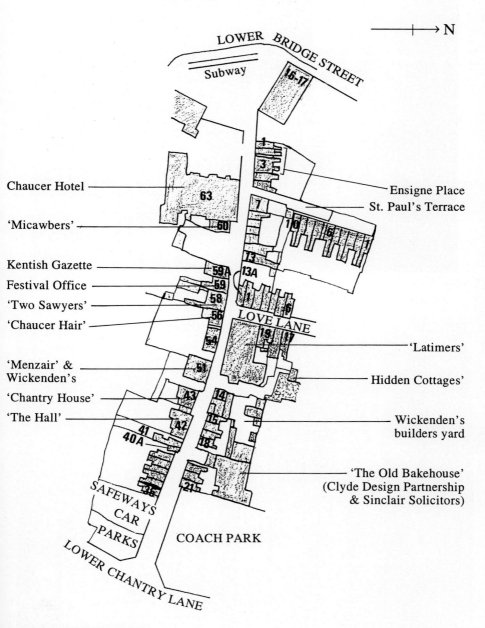

LOWER BRIDGE STREET

Subway

16-17

N

Chaucer Hotel

'Micawbers'

63

60

Ensigne Place
St. Paul's Terrace

4

3

7

10

6

Kentish Gazette
Festival Office
'Two Sawyers'
'Chaucer Hair'

59A
59
58
56

13

13A

1

6

LOVE LANE

'Menzair' &
Wickenden's

'Chantry House'
'The Hall'

54

53

43
42

41
40A

14

15

18

19

17

'Latimers'

Hidden Cottages'

Wickenden's
builders yard

'The Old Bakehouse'
(Clyde Design Partnership
& Sinclair Solicitors)

35

21

SAFEWAYS
CAR
PARKS

COACH PARK

LOWER CHANTRY LANE

CG

No. 54 Ivy Lane - Photo: N Taylor

The Pilch Collard Coal Office - Photo courtesy of Canterbury Museums

barmaid. Besides her own family, there were eleven others living in the house at the time - one boarder and ten lodgers including a hurdlemaker, a whitesmith and bell-hanger, a sawyer, two hawkers and their wives and a boilermaker and a carpenter and their wives - a total of fifteen people, with an age range from eleven to seventy-five years.

It ceased to be a public house in 1903, and was divided into two properties around 1930. At the present time (1994) 'Menzair', hairdressers, have a shop on the ground floor (No.51). Wickenden's the builders are the property owners and have their office at the rear of No. 51A.

Nos. 52-57

Here Nicholas Barton had his house in the 13th century. It was later occupied by John Standfast whose family for a brief time gave their name to the Lane. The house stood back behind a gate with four shops outside on the Lane frontage to the east.

Nos. 53, 54 and 55 Ivy Lane (c1980)
Photo courtesy of Canterbury Museums

In 1975 No. 52 had gone and cottages 53, 54, and 55 stood empty. The owner asked permission to demolish them, but this was refused. By 1978 the cottages were in an advanced state of disrepair and at this point they became the focus of an historic decision. In 1974 legislation gave the City Council new powers to make repairs, and to claim against the owners for the costs involved. The cottages became almost the first in Britain for which these powers operated. Local people were deeply concerned for their fate and the Department of the Environment decided that the cottages contributed significantly to the character of the Lane. Finally in the 1980's the cottages were sold to Mr N Taylor, a veteran of the battle of El Alamein, and former non-executive director of Kent County Newspapers. By 1982/3, Coombs, the builders began the work of rehabilitation. The three dwellings were made into one, retaining the pleasing external appearance of separate dwellings.

Behind this property lay Moss's Square, with a small right of way (now lost) between Nos.55 - 56 that led through to the 'Little Cottages' in the Square. These were built against the back garden of the present No. 54, sometime before 1841, when the census return shows them occupied by five households containing twenty-three people, including thirteen children. The old maps show six cottages, with a pump in front of them, in the middle of Moss's Square. Later census returns show only two or three occupied, with occupants varying from three to twelve. These and the street directories up to 1895, give occupations of householders as varied as painter, turner, shoemaker, bricklayer, brewer's drayman and needlewoman. One of the last occupants was Samuel

Beddow, a horse-collar maker. By the time the 3rd edition Ordnance Survey map was published in 1907 the cottages had disappeared.

No. 56 was for many years a general shop. From 1882 to 1905, the street directories show the shopkeeper to be Mrs C. Hopper, but from 1911 to 1924 it was W.J. Cox. In 1925 Mrs E M Cox had acquired No. 57. In the 1930's both premises were owned by Mr and Mrs F. W. Jewson, and they lived in No.57 continuing the shop in No.56. Eventually they moved upstairs to live and used the double frontage below as the shop. Later after moving from Ivy Lane they continued the two buildings as a lock-up shop and stores. By 1964 they had ceased trading, and by 1968 it was the office of Pilch & Collard, coal merchants. In July 1969 The Samaritans came to Ivy Lane with an office above the coal merchants and a separate entrance numbered 57A. In 1973 they moved to premises across the Lane at No.13A where they remained until March 1990. The shop below what were the offices is the 'Chaucer Hair Salon', the upper part now being a small flat.

Pilch Collard coal bill
Courtesy Joyce Beadle

At this point between 57A and 'The Two Sawyers' is the old boundary marking the administrative division of the Borough of Longport and the City. In fact from here the

56 Ivy Lane, Chaucer Hair Salon former Pilch Collard - Photo: B. A.

The Two Sawyers - Photo: B. A.

demarcation line runs down the middle of Love Lane and then turns east along the centre of Ivy Lane.

No. 58 'The Two Sawyers'

This was licensed in 1784 to Mr Goodban and, according to the St Paul's Register of 1788, Thos. Johncock was the publican. Rigden & Co were the owners from 1866 to 1908. The 1851 census reveals five sawyers living in Ivy Lane, and it is recorded that in 1897 Henry B. Wilson owned and occupied a builder's yard and sawmill to the rear of St George's Place, behind 'The Two Sawyers' so the public house was aptly named.

Elaine Parry was the licensee from 1959 to 1984. After the death of her husband she was helped considerably by her brother-in-law George Ledger. The *Kentish Gazette* 15 June 1984, had this to say:- *"Their time at The Two Sawyers has brought much happiness and comfort to a great many people. To the Gazette they have been the perfect neighbours"*. It was a sentiment endorsed by the residents of the Lane. The present licensee is Paul Wildman who has renovated the interior and is pleased to make it into an old style 'local' serving the community.

Nos. 59 and 59A

When the Abbey lands were granted to the City in 1543 the plot (which also included No. 58) with its messuages, was held by Henry Sym and David Briggs. It later became part of a holding by the Sare family. William Baldock, brewer, owned it in 1788, and it must have been he who built 'The Two Sawyers' circa 1790 and installed John Goodban there as its first landlord.

In 1871 John Southey had the bakery and shop at No. 59 next to Beers Malt house but from about 1880 it was in the hands of two generations of the Dadds family. It was Mr Leonard Dadds who took photographs of two children's street parties which took

Ivy Lane street party celebrating the Coronation of Elizabeth II. Alderman Frank Hooker on Right and Josie Carroll on Right in doorway - Photo courtesy of Violet Davison

Canterbury Festival Office and rear of Kentish Gazette Office - Photo: B. A.

place in Ivy Lane - one celebrating VE-day and the other the Coronation of Queen Elizabeth II.

No. 59 is the Canterbury Festival Office for Marketing and Publicity. The present Director is Mark Deller the well-known counter tenor, and son of the famous Alfred Deller. The Festival Chairman is Peter Williams, the television and film producer, who at one time lived in Dover Street and was a founder member of The Oaten Hill and District Society

From 1929 No. 59A was C B Giles' garage where the Richardsons took their wireless accumulators for recharging. In 1955-58 it was owned by R Harding and was called Ivy Lane Garage. In 1960 it became 'The Chaucer Hotel Garage'. It is now the rear entrance to the Kentish Gazette office and former print works which stretch through to St George's Place. The rest of the malthouse site is a car park for the Chaucer Hotel.

*Ivy Lane street party celebrating VE Day
Photo courtesy Canterbury Museums*

Nos. 60-63

The Chich family held this plot as a garden in 1220. In 1434 there was a barn and garden there called Matterton. A hundred years later in 1543 Stephen Sare had his messuage, a building on the site of the Chaucer Hotel which can be identified on the 17th century maps.

On the 20th June 1741 The *Kentish Post* announced:- *"Edward West who kept the Bull's Head in Burgate is removed from there to Ivey Hall in the parish of St Paul's, Canterbury, which will be the Sign of Admiral Vernon at which place*  *on Monday next, being 22nd instant, will be fought a Cock-match between the Gentlemen of Wincheap and the Gentlemen of St Paul's aforesaid. They shew seven cocks of a side for one Guinea a Battle, and two the odd. Also a Battle Royal for a Peroke of Half a Guinea Value: No Cock to weigh but four pounds eight ounce and to pay one Shilling entrance. NOTE. There will be a free POT".*

Interestingly in the same paper the following news item appeared:- *"By private letter from London there is certain advice of Admiral Vernon being in possession of Carthagena".*

Admiral Vernon was the contemporary hero of the Peninsular War (1739), and had captured Porto Bello, base of the Spanish Revenue vessels. In 1745 he introduced the seamen's ration of 'grog' into the Royal Navy (Rum with three parts water). The name Grog (hence 'groggy') was derived from a grogram cloth cloak worn by the Admiral. There remains a certain mystery as to the whereabouts of Ivey Hall mentioned in the advertisement above. It has not been possible to establish whether this is The Hall (No.42) or Ivey Hall House (No.63), the site of the Ive family home. It is thought that the latter is the most likely site.

William Loftie, a surgeon of Burgate, held the ground from the City towards the end of the 18th century and in 1800 built the house which is now part of the hotel. His rateable value in the St Paul's tythe records went up from £5 p.a. in 1800 to £15 p.a. in 1802. The house was later the home of the Rev. John Edward Massua Molesworth, Vicar of St Paul's from 1829 to his death in 1839.

Census returns from 1841 to 1861 show the site of the present Nos. 60 to 63 (Chaucer Hotel) to be occupied by five houses, Numbered 1 to 5 from Lower Bridge Street. In 1841 a young schoolmaster, Mr William Parker, lived at No. 1 with his wife, two children, four pupils and maidservant, Sarah Key. This house was rented from a Mrs Warren as a temporary home for the first teacher training establishment in Canterbury which was set up by the Diocesan Board of Education in 1840. It remained here only from January 1841 to April 1842, when it moved to permanent premises in the Commercial School at 39 St Margaret's Street. The house was also the home of the Commercial School Master who had charge of Training School pupils who boarded there. The Training School lasted until 1849, when it closed through lack of funds, and it was not until 1962, over one hundred years later that Christ Church College was founded as another Church of England teacher training college in Canterbury. By 1851 No. 63 had become the 'Eagle Tavern' and continued as such until around 1865 when the landlord, William French, moved to The Fox and Hounds (No. 13). It then became a private dwelling 'Ivey Lane House', where John Aris lived with his wife and sister-in-law. Born in 1807 he was an Alderman of the City and Clerk to the Justices in the 19th century. His widow, Susannah, continued to live in the house until she died in 1900.

The other four houses on the site in 1841 also have an interesting history. No. 2 was occupied between 1841 and 1861 by a charwoman and then by a laundress, No. 3 by a bricklayer and then by a smith and No. 4 by a labourer, followed by a general dealer. No. 5, which corresponds to the present No. 60, called 'Micawbers', and now the staff quarters of the Chaucer Hotel, was a pork butcher's shop occupied for nearly forty years by the same family, run first by William Lee and then by his widow, Charlotte, until 1889. From 1871 onwards, there were only four houses (now numbered 60 to 63) the last being Ivy Lane House. From 1891 to 1906 No. 60 was occupied by a laundress, Mrs J French, with five children and two nieces. After a succession of owners it became in 1952 the home of Mrs D. B. Norfolk who lived there until her death, after which the house was acquired by the Chaucer Hotel. Looking at 'Micawbers' now, traces of another door and a wide beam over the window suggest that this may have been the 19th century butcher's shop. The present door can be identified with the original No.61 before the rebuilding in 1957.

No. 61 (previously No. 4) was occupied by George Bennett, a general dealer, and his family, from 1851 to 1871, but in the 1871 census the occupant is given as George Knell, an organ builder. From 1919 to 1939 it was occupied by Mr James Muallis and after the war by Miss B Muallis until the Chaucer Hotel acquired it in 1955. No. 62

(previously No. 3) was occupied by a corn dealer, Mr George Bing, from 1871 to 1889, and then by various private owners, ending with Mr M. Tapley who lived there from 1911 until the 1939-45 war, after which it is no longer listed. The previous No. 2 seems to have disappeared when John Aris came to live in 'Ivy Lane House' in about 1865.

After various other owners and a change of name in 1915 to 'Inglenook', Bakers Temperance Hotel purchased No. 63 in 1934. A pamphlet issued at the time says *"the New Baker's Hotel in Ivy Lane which will be opened on 31 December 1934 consists of a large Private House which has been reconditioned throughout. Many years ago this building was a House of Refreshment and is described in Old Deeds as : 'All that messuage or tenement called the Eagle Tavern with Bowling Green, Gateway, Yard, Garden, Coach House, Shed and Blacksmith's Shop with appurtenances situate in Ivy Lane in the parishes of St Paul and St George in the City of Canterbury' "*.

In 1939 the hotel had thirty-five bedrooms. Bed and breakfast cost 7/6d and a cup of early morning tea was 3d. Prices for luncheon and dinner varied from 2/6d to 3/-s and you could have a hot bath for 1s or a cold one for 6d.

It was in the last years of her life that Mary Tourtel came as a permanent resident to Bakers Temperance Hotel. She was the creator of the first strip cartoon for children to be included in a national newspaper - *The Daily Express*. It featured stories of a bear called Rupert. This cartoon became an instant success. Children of the 1920's looked forward with eagerness to the adventures of Rupert and it still maintains a great popularity. Mary Tourtel died on the 15th March 1948 aged seventy-four. There is a

Ivey Lane House (c1900), now part of Chaucer Hotel - Photo courtesy of Derek Butler

The Chaucer Hotel - Photo: B. A.

commemorative plaque on the wall of the present Chaucer Hotel and her grave may be seen on the terrace of St Martin's churchyard.

In 1955 the Hotel, along with adjoining properties, was acquired by Trust Houses and was doubled in size, re-opening on 29th March 1957 as The Chaucer Hotel. The first managers were Mr and Mrs C. France. Later the hotel became part of Trusthouse Forte, now Forte Hotels.

The present manager is Mr P Wilcock, who for many years has generously allowed the Oaten Hill Society to sing carols in the hotel for local charities. The Chaucer Hotel is proving an attractive place to stay for visitors to the City and also a convenient venue for conferences, weddings, dinner parties and celebrations.

The Rectory of St Martin's and St Paul's

The address of the Rectory was 15 Lower Bridge Street, but is included since the building stood on the corner, and the long Rectory garden sided onto Ivy Lane. In 1882 the house had been occupied by Dr D Barnes, physician and surgeon, but was purchased for use as a Rectory in 1884. As noted in the Parish Magazine:- *"The principal event of the coming year will be the acquisition of the house on the corner of Ivy Lane and Bridge Street as the Rectory. It is many years since an Incumbent of these parishes lived among his people and we have to go further still to find traces of there having been a Rectory House either for St Martin's or St Paul's."* The first Rector to live there was the Rev. L. P. Goodwin. Later occupants include the Rev. Leonard White-Thompson, from 1894 to 1901, and the Rev Ian White-Thompson, his son, 1935 to early 1942, who was to become Dean of Canterbury Cathedral. It was the Rev. G Day who was living there when it was bombed in 1942.

The Rectory would have stood just above the present underpass, whilst the garden occupied all of the land in front of the Chaucer Hotel. Jim Rosseter as a Payne Smith schoolboy (c1911) walked regularly past the Rectory on his way to school, and he gives this description *"... it was quite the ugliest and most massive house in the Victorian Florentine style I have ever seen. It was of solid red brick with gaping segmental headed windows, a frowning front door and machicolations round the parapet! But despite its strength it disappeared in the Blitz".*

LIFE IN THE LANE WITHIN LIVING MEMORY

The poverty between the wars (1918-1939) did little to damp the spirits of the families living in the Lane. With larger families than houses could comfortably accommodate, it was not surprising that life spilled over into the street. Here the children played their games, teased, squabbled, exchanged secrets and made friendships.

Hilda Smithson (nee Gadd) tells us:- *"We went out for perhaps an hour before tea and we were allowed to play hopscotch, marking the pavement with a lump of chalk that my father would bring home for us. When it was time to go in my mother used to call us and we'd bring a bucket of water to wash it all off the pavement."*

Hilda also remembers playing whip and top, girls as well as boys, *"and hoops, us girls had the wooden hoops and all the boys had iron hoops with a hook to bowl them".*

"We played 'Skips in the Lane' - skipping. Then there was Nip Pat - that was a little piece of wood sharpened at each end and you had a stick, you lay the pointed Nip stick on the ground and see who could knock it the farthest."

Alfred Gadd :- *"We'd get the gramophone out from the front room and get the old 78 records on. We also used to play cards, ludo and snap. We had a wonderful home and wonderful parents. We had a coal fire and when we could afford it we bought some bloaters. We hung them on the bars of the fire with a little tray underneath to catch all the drips and we used to roast them and that was a good meal.*

Our lighting was a paraffin lamp. It hung down from the ceiling; you had to be very careful how you turned it up in case you broke the glass."

With little cash to spare holidays were a luxury beyond belief. Alfred Gadd remembers, *"During the school holidays, if we were lucky and mother could afford it, we might get taken to Whitstable for the day or down to Margate.*

The train fare from Canterbury West to Whitstable was 4½d return." Sometimes a good-hearted neighbour would offer to take a child from another family with her own. For this Alfred remembers Mrs Jenner who lived at 19 Ivy Lane. Mrs Jenner was the mother of Mrs Wraight, who gives her own memories in this book. Alfred says of Mrs Richardson who lived at No. 46 (now the garage of The Hall):- *"Mrs Richardson, bless her, she was a lovely lady. She sold potatoes, and all vegetables."*

Ivy Jewson:- *"When I was young I had a halfpenny on Saturday and I remember looking in the sweetshop and wondering what to buy. So many aniseed balls, or a stick of liquorice or one gobstopper - they were enormous things that changed colour as you sucked them you know, and you'd keep looking to see if you'd got to the next colour."*

Emily Pope, nee Deal:- *"After school we had tea round five o'clock, then we went outside to play in the street - we hadn't any gardens but we used to play with hoops and tops, skipping ropes, hopscotch. There was hardly any traffic down the road - only horsedrawn or bicycles. I remember getting knocked down by a bicycle; I came out of my front door one day and stepped off the pavement and a bicycle knocked me down - I wasn't badly hurt".*

Dorothy Wraight was born at No. 19. She lived there for sixty-nine years, and has only recently moved away. She recalls:- *"In the summer we'd go out and play; there were no cars much then to come down small roads like ours. When we heard Bell Harry go at the Cathedral then it was time for us to go in. In the winter when it was cold we would stay in and play or paint."* Of her house she tells us:- *"It was a cottage, there were two rooms downstairs and a kitchen and very narrow winding stairs with two bedrooms. At one time there was six of us. My brother had a bed downstairs, and me being the youngest I was in mother's bedroom. My sisters slept in the other room. There was only gas lighting at our house until I was eleven, then we had electricity. Mother cooked on an open range - it was an open fire with an oven at the side. We had lino on the floor and rugs, of course, but in the sitting room we had a square carpet. My father made all the rugs, they weren't wool ones, those were too expensive, we would have to cut up material into long strips and he made the rugs. They were heavy but they lasted."*

Christmas in the family was vividly remembered. *"We were very fortunate really. My mother had many brothers and sisters and they would come to us at*

Christmas and stay with one or other. Mother would do most of the cooking and I remember that on Christmas morning we had a stocking and an orange, a few nuts, paper puzzle books - only small ones - pencils and perhaps one other toy - maybe a doll that my mother had made and dressed and a shoebox where she'd made pillows and covers and made a cradle for me.

Christmas to us was wonderful because we were all together and we'd have sugar pigs after lunch - the children would go in one room and the adults in another and we'd have sugar pigs, and other little novelties which was a real treat. For Christmas dinner we had chicken which was wonderful because we didn't have chicken often. We always had Christmas pudding - mother made the Christmas puddings and a Christmas cake and mincepies and all things like that. We also had a Christmas tree which my bachelor uncle provided. We made decorations for it - we saved all our toffee papers because they were quite pretty and made butterflies or flowers with them or crepe paper, silver paper too and paper chains - the strip paper chains - then we had to glue them together and link them through. That was started weeks before Christmas.

We played games and sang and we had spoons in bottles to make a noise like a jazz band. In the early days we didn't have a piano. Someone else played a comb with a piece of paper and an auntie could play the harmonica. Mr Oliver played the accordion outside and especially New Year because he was Scottish."

Wash day was Monday and Dorothy Wraight recalls:-
"There was a copper in the kitchen and we had to light the fire and boil the water in the copper. No washing powders, it was just soda and good hard rubbing - very hard on the hands and no rubber gloves then! When the water started to boil then we'd put the clothes in with the copper stick. It was like a small broom handle made of wood, and with it we stirred the clothes round and lifted them out. I never remember my mother having tongs. Washing took all Monday morning. A big mangle was kept in the kitchen behind the door. We were never allowed to touch it because mother was always frightened of us catching our fingers in the rollers. Those mangles were very efficient, if you folded things correctly they almost ironed themselves. The clothes were pegged out on the line in the garden and propped up to get them dry. If it was a wet day the things just had to wait - my mother wouldn't have lines in the kitchen because we were going to and fro all the time, but if we weren't there then she'd put them round the clothes horse and have them round the fire."

There was a special job for every day of the week. *"Mother did the ironing on Tuesdays and clean the windows. She would do the bedrooms one day and another room another day - whiting the copper round - that had to be done every week too, it was a packet of whitening - you put it in a bowl with so much water and you had a brush and brushed all the copper to keep it all nice and clean on the outside. The hearth in front of the fire was always white and the front door step."*

Without a bathroom all personal washing was done in the kitchen. Bath night was once a week. Dorothy Wraight continues:- *"We had a big galvanised tin bath and when it wasn't in use it had to hang on the wall outside. We'd heat all the water in the copper and then bale it into the bath. We had proper balers for that job then, like a shallow tin bowl with a wooden handle. You dipped it in the copper and brought it up full of water and put it in the bath."*

The W.C. was outside. *"It backed on to the kitchen, it was all under the same roof but we had to go out of the back door, walk the length of the kitchen and turn the round corner. To begin with it wasn't a flush type; no, it had to be buckets of water every time it was used. In those days of course the toilets were much different and the seat of the actual toilet was fixed wood and went straight across the top. You couldn't pick the seat up, and that had to be scrubbed - probably twice a week. I was about five when we had a proper flush toilet - it was a boon; we thought it was wonderful."*

Emily Pope, was born at No.15. She speaks of the house. *"It was a small house - two up, two down, and a scullery. My brother slept downstairs in the sitting room when we were all at home, the girls were all upstairs and the youngest one had a cot in my parents' room. Downstairs there was a kitchen at the back and a sitting room and a living room. Then there was the toilet and the coal house outside, and there was a very little garden. The house was lit by gas - later we had electricity put on ourselves. Water was laid on but to get hot water we had a copper. We didn't have any lighting in my bedroom, no lighting at all in the winter so we went to bed with a candle.*

We had no stair rails or anything like that - you just stepped down the stairs. I can remember carrying the baby downstairs lots of times and there was nothing to hold on to."

She continues:- *"My father died when he was fifty. My mother did not go out to work she had plenty to do with all the children. She got us all up and dressed and gave us breakfast. We had porridge quite often and the 'roll boy' (Jock Gardener) came with a basket on each arm with green baize over them and all these lovely hot rolls - two a penny - and he'd ring his bell regularly at quarter to eight every morning. I would go and fetch the milk from Barton Court where the Russells lived and they had quite a herd of cows; the cowman lived near where I am now (Longport)... the dairy was at the back of Barton Court House. We took our jugs or cans and bought our milk straight from the cow - and it was still warm. I did the shopping mostly. We used a little shop in Ivy Lane where the hairdressers is now - there were two houses there, one was the shop and the other the home of the shopkeeper, Mrs Cox. That was a little general shop where we could get a lot of things, but mother dealt with David Greig's mostly."*

She also recalls:- *"In the holidays I looked after the babies and I enjoyed doing that, there was always a baby you know and lots of other children around. The pram was a proper coach-built kind, there was a hood and big wheels.*

I went hop picking with my mother and later I would go to Faversham to my grandmother. I'd go for six weeks in the summer holiday and then I'd go with her hop picking. I was quite a good picker so all the money that I earned I had and with that I bought my clothes for the winter - there'd be a dress and some shoes

and a coat if you were lucky, but we always had something different for Sunday. We didn't wear the same things on Sunday and we always had something new at Easter. In the winter I wore lace up boots for week days and button boots on Sunday. In the summer it was shoes for school and patent shoes with straps on Sunday and white socks. The highlight of the year was the Sunday School outing. We went to Whitstable when I was quite young but when I was older we went to Dungeness - we went by bus - the charabanc sort."

The Richardson sisters (Mrs Violet Davison and Mrs Eileen Davies) tell about their life at No.45:- *"It only had four rooms two up and two down. We had to sleep top and bottom - that was how it was! As we grew we went into the other bedroom".* All cooking was done *"on a range with an oven at the side where mother did all her baking. We would go round to Russell's to collect the skimmed milk and mum would make sour milk bread. Meat puddings were done in a cloth - I would go round to Boarmans the butchers for six pennyworth of pieces of meat and that would make a meat pudding. These meat puddings were put on a big dish and a hole cut in the middle and there was a big jug of gravy and 'help yourself'. It was really lovely. We were brought up also to have bread and dripping. Sometimes mum would make a big spotted dick in a cloth and we'd eat it with custard."*

After the death of their mother the Richardson family went to live at No. 51. There from the front window they looked straight up the yard that was Taylor's seed store. *"We'd sit on the window sill and watch them lower the chain down to take the sacks up to the loft. That fascinated us. There were all these horses and carts. Then there was a builder's yard - Coombs. There were a lot of people working in Ivy Lane. There was Amey's - they made blinds, then there was the Coop bakery, a tailor's, Dadd's bakery - lovely bread there - Mr Ilott, the 'snob' and there* was a garage where we took the accumulators to be charged. We washed in the kitchen sink; it was the only place there was, there was no bathroom in that house and no water upstairs. We had a tin bath that hung outside the kitchen. We bathed in front of the fire. Mum heated the water up in the copper. I think we all went in the same water, two or three of us. But she was very fussy. It was girls one night and boys the other night, and we couldn't peep! Mother was very strict."*

Both girls started school at St Paul's C. of E. School and then went to the Catholic school. Their older brother Bill went to Payne Smith school. The children always went home for dinner. Violet left school just before her fourteenth birthday. She recalls *"I left because Dad got permission for me to leave early to look after Paddy because he was a mongol. He died when he was five, but in a way it was a happy release. So I left*

school at thirteen and a half."

Eileen remembers the Kent and Canterbury Hospital when it was in Longport. *"See I got a scar there? I was playing with the boys in Ivy Lane running and I banged into the corner where my Auntie Josie's house was and I cut my eye open, so I was taken over to the old hospital. There were two sisters, one in the maternity and the other in charge of casualty and I remember these stitches going in, no sympathy you know, 'you shouldn't have been playing with the boys' she said. Aunt Josie worked there, making beds, doing cleaning. Miss Annie Purchas was the matron. The nurses home was in Longport just opposite the hospital but that got bombed."* Violet also remembers the hospital. *"I can remember going there once to have my tonsils out and I couldn't have been very old because Mum had me in a pushchair and she pushed me there and she got to the front door, but then she changed her mind and brought me home again. I've still got my tonsils."*

The sisters remember their neighbours:- *"Mrs Gadd, Mrs Jenner, Mrs Coulton, Mrs Crunden, they all lived in that row of houses for years and years and nobody else lived there so you always knew where to go. And as their children grew up they took over the houses, like we did."*

Stove with flat irons
Photo courtesy of W Smith

Hilda Smithson lived at 39 Ivy Lane; she left school at fourteen:- *"My mother took me up to the Beaumont Hand Laundry in London Road and I got a job there. I first worked sorting the washing but later I went on to the ironing - piece work. I did surplices for the Cathedral and I'd get a penny for ironing one and it took ages because they were all starched. Shirts - you'd get a farthing for them. Only the ironing was piecework. We used flat irons and had a big combustion stove to heat the irons, and the irons were all round the side. I earned about five shillings a week, if I'd done well on piecework I'd earn another shilling or so."*

Her memory of the street in the twenties:- *" Gas lighting - it was late before we had electricity in the Lane. I can remember the man coming round and pulling the light on. There were road sweepers who came down the Lane, and after it had been swept the water cart would come spraying to wash the ground - the water would spray right across the road and us children would run through it - we had a lot of fun. On Monday the fishman came with his horse and cart.*

He came from Whitstable, he'd scoop the fish from a big tray out of the back of the cart, it was always nice and fresh. Tuesdays and Wednesdays the rag and bone man came along, we'd take a few rags out to him and get a goldfish. There was a man who was a poacher who lived in Union Row, he'd come home and have a string of rabbits all round his neck, round his waist and all round his legs, he had a job to walk. My mother would send me to him to buy a rabbit. They were about twopence or threepence. In the early days there were ten of us in the family but my mother lost four when they were very young. I can remember somebody being taken away from Ivy Lane - one of our school mates - who had diptheria. She was taken to the fever hospital at Stodmarsh in a big black cab. Then they fumigated the house before anyone was allowed back in."

In the 1930's when Mr and Mrs Jewson married they took over the shop at No. 56 from Mrs Cox. Mrs Jewson describes how it was:- *"It was an old-fashioned shop just in the front room and there was sacking on the floor and the window had goods in it but all caged in - almost like a rabbit hutch with netting frames. We just sold tea, sugar, mustard, paraffin, faggots and coal. We didn't sell bread because Mr Dadds, the baker, was just two doors down. We soon altered the shop - opened it more as a general store. We opened at eight o'clock in the morning and stayed open until eight at night."* Restrictions on goods sold on Sundays and after hours were a source of fear. *"I was terribly frightened in those days - it was odd, but you could sell some things but not others and of course, people would come round the back door or after eight o'clock at night - no matter how late you stayed open it was never late enough for some people. We soon stopped selling paraffin and coal and faggots and enlarged the business. It meant buying in bulk. We had to weigh everything and put it into bags. We made up 1lb and 2lbs of sugar and flour in 3lbs. Sugar was always in a blue bag and soda in a brown bag. A lot of people were really hard up, quite a lot of them got tick. One young man I met later said to me 'I always remember you - we'd have been hungry very often if it hadn't been for you and Mr Jewson being so understanding to Mother'. In those days if they wanted help they weren't given money but vouchers and we were told what to supply for the voucher - so much oatmeal and really horrible basic things - we used to stretch it a bit sometimes and give them something else to the same value."*

During the war Mr Jewson went into the forces and Mrs Jewson and family were evacuated. During this time Mr Gann took over the shop. He already had a shop in Nunnery Fields. When they returned after the war they carried on for a bit, then gave up the shop in Ivy Lane.

THE WAR YEARS 1939-1945

Immediately outside the City walls it was South Canterbury that suffered most in the local air raids. The biggest raid on the City was on the night of May 31 - June 1 1942. One hundred and thirty high explosive bombs, including five delayed action bombs, and 3,600 incendiary bombs were dropped. A stiff breeze that night blew the marker flares to the south of the City, and many of the loads intended for the inner City fell instead to the South. It was said to be a reprisal raid for the allied bombing of Cologne. These raids on historic cities became known as 'Baedeker' raids.

The spaces at either side of Ivy Lane at the Junction with Lower Chantry Lane provide evident scars of the damage. More than thirteen houses were destroyed or damaged beyond repair in Ivy Lane alone. At the City end the St Paul's Rectory in Lower Bridge Street was very severely damaged, victim of a large bomb that fell at the Junction of St George's Place and St George's Street. All of the properties on the north side of St George's Place, backing onto the Lane were destroyed, mostly by incendiaries.

Archie Waters told us *"The greatest bomb of all, the greatest incident in this area, was a bomb dropped on the hard surface of Lower Chantry Lane, and with that and the fire, destroyed the Payne Smith School* (facing Lower Chantry Lane and siding onto Ivy Lane). *All the little houses in Lower Chantry Lane went. The Payne Smith School after it was hit was just a mess, a mass of rubble."*

Dorothy Wraight has this memory of the raid:- *"We were in Ivy Lane and my brother had put a dugout in the garden - we'd done it ourselves. He was in the Air Force and he was home on leave and the man next door but one he was an ARP warden and he was on his own and my brother said to him 'I'll come and sit with you rather than know you're on your own'. My sister was staying with us and she had a little boy, he was about two or three and we went down into the shelter in the garden and we'd just got down there when the bombs started dropping and they were all round us - it was terrible. The noise was deafening. That afternoon we'd been out and bought this little boy his first overcoat. It was new, he'd never worn it.*

My brother came running up and said 'They're dropping flares, go down into the dugout as quickly as possible'. We grabbed the little boy plus the overcoat we'd just bought and it was cold so we put this over-coat on him and as he stood by my mother, 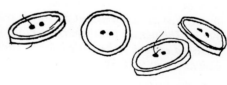 *he must have kept twisting these buttons because when we came out of the dugout there wasn't a button left on the coat. He'd got so nervous and had to keep fiddling and we found all these buttons on the floor of the shelter.*

When we came up we found the windows smashed and the front door had blown open. The front of the piano was blown across the room. All the curtains was torn and the mess was terrible, there seemed to be soot everywhere. And then we walked along the road and outside Payne Smith School they'd a lot of coal and that was all alight. There was no water so we had to go to the standpipes with the firemen and we boiled the kettles on all this coal to make drinks - that was in the boys' playground at the top of Ivy Lane. The school was just ablaze. There was too much smoke and smell to really take in what was happening. We went across to the old hospital that was then in Longport and they were making soup and tea."

Violet Richardson was twelve when the War started in September 1939. Their mother died in the December of the same year. Sister Eileen was sixteen and found it all rather exciting. She says *"We would watch the 'dog fights' and men jumping out and we weren't frightened at all. I remember when I got married, there was a little row of cottages, near where Safeways is now - a row of about six cottages. Well, I put in for one of them and we got it, that was fifteen shillings a week rent. It was No.2 Chantry Lane. My husband came home on leave and I was four months gone with Carol then and I'd bought baby clothes like you do. Well, we lived there and my husband had gone back, so I went to my father's and that was the weekend of the bombing in June 1942. Violet slept like a log and I ran upstairs to wake her up 'quick, quick, there's bombing' and she was only banging on the wall and trying to get through the wall and I said 'Look there's the door' and we looked out of the window and there were all these pretty lights coming down - then fire bombs - and for a minute I couldn't register what was happening. And I was under the table* (No.51 Ivy Lane) *and there was Granny Carroll and Granny Richardson and my Auntie Josie all on top of me, trying to hide me because I was pregnant. When we managed to get out there were fires all round, everywhere, we were within a ball of fire. The top half of the town was just flattened. All St George's Street was down. Ivy Lane stood on its own in the middle of it... It just didn't seem to register - it didn't frighten us, you just accepted it."* Anxiety made Eileen eager to see her own house in Chantry Lane and she found that - *"the shrapnel had gone right through the whole roof and if my husband and I had been in bed there was pieces of shrapnel right across the pillow and the baby clothes that had been left on the bed. Well I never did get them. After that it was all boarded up and all my wedding presents. Payne Smith school was taken down afterwards, and the corner of Longport, that went. When I came up to look at my place I looked across here and this exact row of houses by there was a tree and I remember seeing this German, either a pilot or a gunner, dead with no legs, hanging from the tree. Our houses weren't demolished at that time but they were pulled down afterwards as they weren't fit to live in. The houses in St George's Place weren't completely destroyed but they were damaged enough to be pulled down. Then for a long time it was just an open space with tall trees until Safeways was built."*

In the back garden of No. 37 where Mrs Hilda Smithson lived there was a large shelter. It had been built by Mr Smithson and a neighbour. It was sunk into the ground and built of brick, with a door at either end. It had a small coke-burning stove and a flue that went up through the roof of the shelter. On the night of 31 May/1 June there were forty-two people in the shelter. Hilda tells us *"When the bomb dropped in Lower Chantry Lane the doors of the shelter blew right off and were found in the garden. Hearing shouting, we went into Ivy Lane and found the ARP warden, Mr Hudson from No. 16, lying on the garden path. He had been injured from shrapnel and his leg was cut right open. The men got the door from the path and put him on it and carried him to the emergency First Aid Post which was in the Co-op bakery in Ivy Lane."*

The following appeared in St George's Parish magazine, June 1942:-

"On Saturday a further raid of one and a half hours took place; this time the barrage from our AA guns was tremendous. The sky was full of every kind of bursting shell, rocket and tracer bullets. Nevertheless, bombs were dropped at the junction of Ivy Lane and Lower Bridge Street. The Rector of St Martin's and St Paul's and his wife, the Rev. and Mrs G Day, had a narrow escape, the bomb exploding five yards from them and bringing part of the Rectory down on them."

The only pre-war building left in Lower Chantry Lane is the Cooper and Adkinson Almshouses. On the night of the 21 January 1944 both Ivy Lane and the Almshouses had a narrow escape when during an air raid a JU 88 crashed.

Mrs Wickenden tells of this occasion:- *"I was on fire-watch duty and I heard a plane come down. I thought it was a British plane and ran along Ivy Lane towards Chantry Lane, where it had crashed. My idea was to run to the rescue of the crew. As I ran, two men ran towards me, on reaching me they came either side of me and putting an arm each through mine picked me up bodily. I found myself going backwards; my feet not touching the ground and being propelled away from the wreck. The next moment there was a loud explosion and we found ourselves in a heap on the ground. The men had saved my life, for had I gone on, I would have received the full blast from the exploding bombs on the German plane."*

The "END" of a Ju 88

THIS RAIDER WAS SHOT DOWN AND CRASHED IN THE MIDDLE OF A SOUTH-EAST TOWN. The picture shows the severed tail fin.

Crashed JU88 - Photo: Kentish Gazette

The *Kentish Herald*, Wednesday 26 January, reported the incident as follows:-

"...following a sharp burst of A.A. fire watchers saw the plane catch fire when it was apparently hit. Rapidly losing height, it hurtled across the sky like a ball of fire, narrowly missing the roofs of houses before it crashed and burst with a terrific explosion which rocked nearby houses.... The wreckage was scattered over a considerable area. One engine landed in the middle of a road and the other in the front garden of some almshouses....Four or five Nazi airmen perished. One had apparently attempted to bale out, but left it too late. When dawn broke he was seen dangling at the end of his parachute which had caught on a gable of the almshouses. He was decapitated."

The dangers and hardships of the War were met by the people of the Lane with fortitude and courage and above all with good humour. The friendly community was beginning to be scattered by the fortunes of war, men were away in the Forces, young women called up, children evacuated, bombed families re-housed. Those remaining grew closer, all knew that life in the Lane would never be the same again

NEVER TO BE THE SAME AGAIN

This has a mournful ring that is reflected in the desolation of the coach park and Safeway's staff car park at the war-torn end of the Lane. This historic thoroughfare deserves a kinder fate. We are hopeful that cottages will be built on these sites in the near future.

Each age creates something for itself. Occupants are no longer bound together by the same poverty, but by a new feeling towards the accessibility of a better quality of life. The little domestic shops in Ivy Lane have gone and the two hairdressers signal a change in trade. Spruce little houses, smart cottages, and demure terraces have emerged. Tarmac has covered the debris of war and modern infill and renovation have in places given the Lane a jaunty air.

On the pleasant green in front of the Chaucer Hotel is a fine cherry tree, near which is a memorial seat. The seat was placed there by the Oaten Hill and District Society to commemorate Cecilia Coomber, Treasurer of the Society from 1977 to 1982. The *Kentish Gazette*, 14 January 1977, published an article headed "Corner that wants to be a Village" featuring Miss Coomber and her memories of the locality. Other early members of the Oaten Hill Society were Dr William Urry, John Farrar, and James Hobbs, alas no longer with us. To them we owe a debt of gratitude for all they did for the local community. Happily they are succeeded by others who still seek to find what is best in the new and to save and preserve treasures of the past. May the harmony of the two be a pleasure for us now and for those to come.

The Oaten Hill Memorial Seat for Celia Coomber - Photo: D Hughes

Ivy Lane looking East - Photo: Colin Graham